50 Ultimate Italian Pasta Cookbook Dishes

By: Kelly Johnson

Table of Contents

- Spaghetti Carbonara
- Fettuccine Alfredo
- Lasagna Bolognese
- Penne Arrabbiata
- Cacio e Pepe
- Pasta Primavera
- Pesto Genovese with Trofie
- Bucatini all'Amatriciana
- Tagliatelle al Ragù (Bolognese)
- Spaghetti Aglio e Olio
- Orecchiette with Broccoli Rabe and Sausage
- Ravioli di Ricotta e Spinaci with Butter Sage Sauce
- Linguine alle Vongole (Clam Pasta)
- Pasta e Fagioli (Pasta and Bean Soup)
- Fregola with Seafood
- Gnocchi alla Sorrentina
- Tortellini in Brodo (Tortellini in Broth)
- Pappardelle al Cinghiale (Wild Boar Ragu)
- Penne alla Vodka
- Spaghetti alle Cozze (Mussels Pasta)
- Maccheroni al Forno (Baked Macaroni)
- Strozzapreti with Sausage and Fennel
- Farfalle with Smoked Salmon and Cream
- Rigatoni alla Norma (Eggplant and Tomato Sauce)
- Tagliolini al Tartufo (Truffle Pasta)
- Casarecce with Sun-Dried Tomatoes and Olives
- Cannelloni with Ricotta and Spinach
- Ziti al Forno (Baked Ziti)
- Stracci with Porcini Mushrooms
- Tonnarelli Cacio e Pepe with Black Truffle
- Fusilli with Pesto and Cherry Tomatoes
- Paccheri with Swordfish and Capers
- Vermicelli with Bottarga (Cured Fish Roe)
- Pici all'Aglione (Garlic Tomato Sauce)
- Penne with Gorgonzola and Walnuts

- Fettuccine with Wild Mushrooms
- Calamarata Pasta with Calamari and Tomato Sauce
- Ravioli with Pumpkin and Amaretti
- Spaghetti alla Puttanesca
- Busiate with Pesto Trapanese (Sicilian Almond Pesto)
- Tagliatelle with Lemon and Shrimp
- Cappelletti in Brodo (Stuffed Pasta in Broth)
- Linguine with Lobster Sauce
- Casunziei (Beet Ravioli from Veneto)
- Gramigna with Sausage and Saffron Cream
- Tortellini alla Panna (Creamy Tortellini)
- Fusilli with Ricotta and Zucchini
- Agnolotti del Plin (Stuffed Pasta from Piedmont)
- Lasagna al Pesto
- Pasta alla Gricia (Pecorino and Guanciale)

Spaghetti Carbonara

Ingredients:

- 12 oz spaghetti
- 4 oz pancetta, diced
- 2 eggs + 1 egg yolk
- ½ cup grated Pecorino Romano
- ½ teaspoon black pepper

Instructions:

1. Cook spaghetti until al dente. Reserve ½ cup pasta water.
2. Sauté pancetta until crispy.
3. Whisk eggs, cheese, and black pepper.
4. Toss pasta with pancetta, remove from heat, then mix in egg mixture, adding pasta water to create a creamy sauce.

Fettuccine Alfredo

Ingredients:

- 12 oz fettuccine
- ½ cup butter
- 1 cup heavy cream
- 1 cup Parmesan cheese, grated
- ½ teaspoon black pepper

Instructions:

1. Cook fettuccine until al dente.
2. Melt butter in a pan, then add heavy cream. Simmer for 2 minutes.
3. Stir in Parmesan and black pepper, then toss with pasta.

Lasagna Bolognese

Ingredients:

- 12 lasagna sheets
- 1 lb ground beef
- 1 small onion, diced
- 1 carrot, diced
- 1 can (28 oz) crushed tomatoes
- 1 cup béchamel sauce
- 1 cup Parmesan cheese
- 1 tablespoon olive oil

Instructions:

1. Sauté onion, carrot, and beef in olive oil. Add tomatoes and simmer for 30 minutes.
2. Layer pasta, Bolognese sauce, béchamel, and Parmesan in a baking dish.
3. Repeat layers and bake at 375°F (190°C) for 45 minutes.

Penne Arrabbiata

Ingredients:

- 12 oz penne
- 2 cloves garlic, minced
- 1 teaspoon red pepper flakes
- 1 can (14 oz) diced tomatoes
- 2 tablespoons olive oil
- ¼ cup chopped parsley

Instructions:

1. Cook penne until al dente.
2. Sauté garlic and red pepper flakes in olive oil. Add tomatoes and simmer for 15 minutes.
3. Toss with pasta and garnish with parsley.

Cacio e Pepe

Ingredients:

- 12 oz spaghetti
- 1 cup Pecorino Romano, grated
- 1 teaspoon black pepper
- ½ cup pasta water

Instructions:

1. Cook spaghetti until al dente.
2. Toast black pepper in a dry pan, then add pasta water.
3. Toss pasta with cheese and black pepper, stirring until creamy.

Pasta Primavera

Ingredients:

- 12 oz pasta (linguine or penne)
- 1 zucchini, sliced
- 1 bell pepper, sliced
- 1 cup cherry tomatoes, halved
- 1 tablespoon olive oil
- ½ cup Parmesan cheese

Instructions:

1. Cook pasta until al dente.
2. Sauté vegetables in olive oil until tender.
3. Toss with pasta and Parmesan.

Pesto Genovese with Trofie

Ingredients:

- 12 oz trofie pasta
- 2 cups fresh basil
- ¼ cup pine nuts
- 2 cloves garlic
- ½ cup Parmesan cheese, grated
- ½ cup olive oil

Instructions:

1. Cook trofie pasta until al dente.
2. Blend basil, pine nuts, garlic, cheese, and olive oil into a pesto sauce.
3. Toss with pasta before serving.

Bucatini all'Amatriciana

Ingredients:

- 12 oz bucatini
- 4 oz guanciale, diced
- 1 can (14 oz) crushed tomatoes
- ½ teaspoon red pepper flakes
- ½ cup Pecorino Romano, grated

Instructions:

1. Cook bucatini until al dente.
2. Sauté guanciale until crispy, then add tomatoes and red pepper flakes.
3. Toss with pasta and Pecorino Romano.

Tagliatelle al Ragù (Bolognese)

Ingredients:

- 12 oz tagliatelle
- 1 lb ground beef
- 1 small onion, diced
- 1 carrot, diced
- 1 can (28 oz) crushed tomatoes
- 1 cup beef broth
- ½ cup red wine

Instructions:

1. Sauté onion, carrot, and beef until browned.
2. Add tomatoes, broth, and wine, then simmer for 1 hour.
3. Toss with tagliatelle and serve.

Spaghetti Aglio e Olio

Ingredients:

- 12 oz spaghetti
- 4 cloves garlic, sliced
- ¼ teaspoon red pepper flakes
- ¼ cup olive oil
- ¼ cup parsley, chopped

Instructions:

1. Cook spaghetti until al dente.
2. Sauté garlic and red pepper flakes in olive oil.
3. Toss with pasta and parsley.

Orecchiette with Broccoli Rabe and Sausage

Ingredients:

- 12 oz orecchiette
- 1 bunch broccoli rabe, chopped
- ½ lb Italian sausage, crumbled
- 2 cloves garlic, minced
- 2 tablespoons olive oil
- ½ teaspoon red pepper flakes

Instructions:

1. Cook orecchiette until al dente.
2. Sauté sausage in olive oil, then add garlic and red pepper flakes.
3. Add broccoli rabe and cook until tender. Toss with pasta.

Ravioli di Ricotta e Spinaci with Butter Sage Sauce

Ingredients:

- **For the ravioli:**
    - 2 cups all-purpose flour
    - 2 eggs
    - 1 teaspoon olive oil
    - ½ teaspoon salt
- **For the filling:**
    - 1 cup ricotta cheese
    - ½ cup cooked spinach, chopped
    - ¼ cup Parmesan cheese, grated
    - 1 egg yolk
    - ½ teaspoon nutmeg
- **For the sauce:**
    - 4 tablespoons butter
    - 6 fresh sage leaves

Instructions:

1. Make pasta dough by mixing flour, eggs, olive oil, and salt. Knead and rest for 30 minutes.
2. Roll out the dough and cut into ravioli squares.
3. Mix ricotta, spinach, Parmesan, egg yolk, and nutmeg for the filling.
4. Place filling on pasta sheets, seal, and cut into ravioli.
5. Boil ravioli for 3 minutes.
6. Melt butter in a pan with sage leaves, then toss with ravioli.

Linguine alle Vongole (Clam Pasta)

Ingredients:

- 12 oz linguine
- 1 lb fresh clams, cleaned
- 2 cloves garlic, minced
- ½ teaspoon red pepper flakes
- ½ cup white wine
- 2 tablespoons olive oil
- ¼ cup chopped parsley

Instructions:

1. Cook linguine until al dente.
2. Sauté garlic and red pepper flakes in olive oil.
3. Add clams and white wine, cover, and steam until clams open.
4. Toss with pasta and parsley.

Pasta e Fagioli (Pasta and Bean Soup)

Ingredients:

- 1 cup ditalini pasta
- 1 can cannellini beans, drained
- 1 small onion, diced
- 2 cloves garlic, minced
- 1 can diced tomatoes
- 4 cups vegetable broth
- 1 teaspoon oregano
- 1 tablespoon olive oil

Instructions:

1. Sauté onion and garlic in olive oil.
2. Add tomatoes, beans, broth, and oregano. Simmer for 20 minutes.
3. Stir in pasta and cook until tender.

Fregola with Seafood

Ingredients:

- 1 cup fregola (Sardinian toasted pasta)
- ½ lb shrimp, peeled
- ½ lb mussels, cleaned
- 1 can diced tomatoes
- 2 cloves garlic, minced
- ½ cup white wine
- 2 tablespoons olive oil

Instructions:

1. Sauté garlic in olive oil. Add tomatoes and white wine, simmer for 5 minutes.
2. Add shrimp and mussels, cover, and cook until mussels open.
3. Cook fregola separately, then toss with seafood mixture.

Gnocchi alla Sorrentina

Ingredients:

- 1 lb potato gnocchi
- 2 cups tomato sauce
- 1 cup mozzarella, cubed
- ¼ cup Parmesan cheese, grated
- 1 tablespoon olive oil
- ½ teaspoon basil

Instructions:

1. Cook gnocchi until they float.
2. Toss with tomato sauce, mozzarella, and basil.
3. Transfer to a baking dish, sprinkle with Parmesan, and broil until bubbly.

Tortellini in Brodo (Tortellini in Broth)

Ingredients:

- 12 oz fresh tortellini (cheese or meat-filled)
- 4 cups chicken or beef broth
- 1 bay leaf
- ¼ teaspoon black pepper

Instructions:

1. Heat broth with bay leaf and black pepper.
2. Add tortellini and cook for 5 minutes.
3. Serve hot with grated Parmesan.

Pappardelle al Cinghiale (Wild Boar Ragu)

Ingredients:

- 12 oz pappardelle
- 1 lb wild boar, cubed
- 1 small onion, diced
- 1 carrot, diced
- 2 cloves garlic, minced
- 1 cup red wine
- 1 can diced tomatoes
- 1 teaspoon rosemary
- 1 tablespoon olive oil

Instructions:

1. Sauté onion, carrot, and garlic in olive oil.
2. Add wild boar and brown.
3. Stir in wine, tomatoes, and rosemary, then simmer for 2 hours.
4. Toss with pappardelle before serving.

Penne alla Vodka

Ingredients:

- 12 oz penne
- 1 can (14 oz) crushed tomatoes
- ½ cup heavy cream
- ¼ cup vodka
- 1 small onion, diced
- 2 tablespoons olive oil
- ½ teaspoon red pepper flakes

Instructions:

1. Sauté onion and red pepper flakes in olive oil.
2. Add vodka and cook for 2 minutes.
3. Stir in tomatoes and simmer for 15 minutes.
4. Add cream, toss with pasta, and serve.

Spaghetti alle Cozze (Mussels Pasta)

Ingredients:

- 12 oz spaghetti
- 1 lb mussels, cleaned
- 2 cloves garlic, minced
- ½ teaspoon red pepper flakes
- ½ cup white wine
- 2 tablespoons olive oil
- ¼ cup chopped parsley

Instructions:

1. Cook spaghetti until al dente.
2. Sauté garlic and red pepper flakes in olive oil.
3. Add mussels and wine, cover, and cook until mussels open.
4. Toss with pasta and parsley.

Maccheroni al Forno (Baked Macaroni)

Ingredients:

- 12 oz macaroni
- 2 cups tomato sauce
- 1 cup mozzarella, cubed
- ½ cup Parmesan cheese, grated
- 1 tablespoon olive oil
- ½ teaspoon oregano

Instructions:

1. Cook macaroni until al dente.
2. Toss with tomato sauce, mozzarella, and oregano.
3. Transfer to a baking dish, sprinkle with Parmesan, and bake at 375°F (190°C) for 25 minutes.

Strozzapreti with Sausage and Fennel

Ingredients:

- 12 oz strozzapreti pasta
- ½ lb Italian sausage, crumbled
- 1 small fennel bulb, thinly sliced
- 2 cloves garlic, minced
- ½ teaspoon red pepper flakes
- ½ cup white wine
- 2 tablespoons olive oil
- ¼ cup Parmesan cheese, grated

Instructions:

1. Cook strozzapreti until al dente.
2. Sauté sausage in olive oil until browned. Add fennel, garlic, and red pepper flakes.
3. Deglaze with white wine and simmer for 5 minutes.
4. Toss with pasta and top with Parmesan.

Farfalle with Smoked Salmon and Cream

Ingredients:

- 12 oz farfalle pasta
- 4 oz smoked salmon, chopped
- 1 cup heavy cream
- 1 small onion, diced
- 1 tablespoon butter
- ½ teaspoon black pepper
- ¼ cup Parmesan cheese

Instructions:

1. Cook farfalle until al dente.
2. Sauté onion in butter until soft. Add heavy cream and simmer for 2 minutes.
3. Stir in smoked salmon and black pepper.
4. Toss with pasta and sprinkle with Parmesan.

Rigatoni alla Norma (Eggplant and Tomato Sauce)

Ingredients:

- 12 oz rigatoni
- 1 small eggplant, cubed
- 1 can (14 oz) diced tomatoes
- 2 cloves garlic, minced
- ½ teaspoon red pepper flakes
- 2 tablespoons olive oil
- ¼ cup ricotta salata, grated
- ¼ cup fresh basil

Instructions:

1. Cook rigatoni until al dente.
2. Sauté eggplant in olive oil until soft. Add garlic, red pepper flakes, and tomatoes. Simmer for 15 minutes.
3. Toss with pasta and top with ricotta salata and basil.

Tagliolini al Tartufo (Truffle Pasta)

Ingredients:

- 12 oz tagliolini pasta
- 2 tablespoons butter
- ½ teaspoon black truffle oil
- ¼ cup Parmesan cheese, grated
- Black truffle shavings (optional)

Instructions:

1. Cook tagliolini until al dente.
2. Melt butter and mix in truffle oil.
3. Toss with pasta and Parmesan.
4. Garnish with black truffle shavings if available.

Casarecce with Sun-Dried Tomatoes and Olives

Ingredients:

- 12 oz casarecce pasta
- ½ cup sun-dried tomatoes, chopped
- ½ cup Kalamata olives, sliced
- 2 cloves garlic, minced
- 2 tablespoons olive oil
- ¼ teaspoon red pepper flakes
- ¼ cup Parmesan cheese

Instructions:

1. Cook casarecce until al dente.
2. Sauté garlic in olive oil, then add sun-dried tomatoes and olives.
3. Toss with pasta and red pepper flakes.
4. Sprinkle with Parmesan before serving.

Cannelloni with Ricotta and Spinach

Ingredients:

- 12 cannelloni pasta tubes
- 1 cup ricotta cheese
- ½ cup cooked spinach, chopped
- ¼ cup Parmesan cheese
- 1 egg
- 1 teaspoon nutmeg
- 2 cups tomato sauce
- 1 cup mozzarella cheese, shredded

Instructions:

1. Mix ricotta, spinach, Parmesan, egg, and nutmeg. Stuff into cannelloni.
2. Spread tomato sauce in a baking dish, place cannelloni on top, and cover with more sauce.
3. Sprinkle with mozzarella and bake at 375°F (190°C) for 30 minutes.

Ziti al Forno (Baked Ziti)

Ingredients:

- 12 oz ziti pasta
- 2 cups tomato sauce
- 1 cup ricotta cheese
- 1 cup mozzarella cheese, shredded
- ½ cup Parmesan cheese, grated
- 1 teaspoon oregano

Instructions:

1. Cook ziti until al dente.
2. Toss with tomato sauce, ricotta, and oregano.
3. Transfer to a baking dish, top with mozzarella and Parmesan.
4. Bake at 375°F (190°C) for 25 minutes.

Stracci with Porcini Mushrooms

Ingredients:

- 12 oz stracci pasta
- 1 cup porcini mushrooms, sliced
- 2 cloves garlic, minced
- ½ cup heavy cream
- 2 tablespoons olive oil
- ¼ cup Parmesan cheese

Instructions:

1. Cook stracci pasta until al dente.
2. Sauté mushrooms and garlic in olive oil.
3. Stir in heavy cream and Parmesan.
4. Toss with pasta and serve.

Tonnarelli Cacio e Pepe with Black Truffle

Ingredients:

- 12 oz tonnarelli pasta
- 1 teaspoon black pepper
- 1 cup Pecorino Romano, grated
- ½ teaspoon black truffle oil
- ½ cup pasta water

Instructions:

1. Cook tonnarelli until al dente.
2. Toast black pepper in a dry pan, then add pasta water.
3. Toss pasta with cheese, pepper, and truffle oil.

Fusilli with Pesto and Cherry Tomatoes

Ingredients:

- 12 oz fusilli pasta
- 1 cup cherry tomatoes, halved
- ½ cup basil pesto
- ¼ cup Parmesan cheese

Instructions:

1. Cook fusilli until al dente.
2. Toss with pesto and cherry tomatoes.
3. Sprinkle with Parmesan before serving.

Paccheri with Swordfish and Capers

Ingredients:

- 12 oz paccheri pasta
- ½ lb swordfish, cubed
- 1 small onion, diced
- 2 cloves garlic, minced
- 1 can diced tomatoes
- 1 tablespoon capers
- 2 tablespoons olive oil

Instructions:

1. Cook paccheri until al dente.
2. Sauté onion, garlic, and swordfish in olive oil.
3. Add tomatoes and capers, simmer for 10 minutes.
4. Toss with pasta before serving.

Vermicelli with Bottarga (Cured Fish Roe)

Ingredients:

- 12 oz vermicelli pasta
- 2 tablespoons olive oil
- 1 clove garlic, minced
- ½ teaspoon red pepper flakes
- 1 ounce bottarga, grated
- 1 tablespoon lemon zest
- ¼ cup chopped parsley

Instructions:

1. Cook vermicelli until al dente.
2. Sauté garlic and red pepper flakes in olive oil.
3. Toss pasta with garlic oil, bottarga, lemon zest, and parsley.

Pici all'Aglione (Garlic Tomato Sauce)

Ingredients:

- 12 oz pici pasta
- 4 cloves garlic, minced
- 1 can (14 oz) diced tomatoes
- ½ teaspoon red pepper flakes
- 2 tablespoons olive oil
- ¼ teaspoon salt
- ¼ cup fresh basil

Instructions:

1. Cook pici until al dente.
2. Sauté garlic in olive oil, then add tomatoes, red pepper flakes, and salt. Simmer for 15 minutes.
3. Toss with pasta and garnish with basil.

Penne with Gorgonzola and Walnuts

Ingredients:

- 12 oz penne pasta
- ½ cup Gorgonzola cheese, crumbled
- ½ cup heavy cream
- ½ cup walnuts, toasted and chopped
- 2 tablespoons butter
- ¼ teaspoon black pepper

Instructions:

1. Cook penne until al dente.
2. Melt butter and stir in cream and Gorgonzola until smooth.
3. Toss with pasta and walnuts.

Fettuccine with Wild Mushrooms

Ingredients:

- 12 oz fettuccine
- 1 cup mixed wild mushrooms, sliced
- 2 cloves garlic, minced
- ½ cup heavy cream
- 2 tablespoons olive oil
- ¼ cup Parmesan cheese

Instructions:

1. Cook fettuccine until al dente.
2. Sauté mushrooms and garlic in olive oil.
3. Stir in cream and Parmesan, then toss with pasta.

Calamarata Pasta with Calamari and Tomato Sauce

Ingredients:

- 12 oz calamarata pasta
- ½ lb calamari, sliced into rings
- 1 can diced tomatoes
- 2 cloves garlic, minced
- ½ teaspoon red pepper flakes
- ½ cup white wine
- 2 tablespoons olive oil

Instructions:

1. Cook calamarata pasta until al dente.
2. Sauté garlic and red pepper flakes in olive oil. Add calamari and white wine, cooking for 2 minutes.
3. Stir in tomatoes and simmer for 10 minutes.
4. Toss with pasta before serving.

Ravioli with Pumpkin and Amaretti

Ingredients:

- 12 oz fresh pumpkin ravioli
- 4 tablespoons butter
- 6 fresh sage leaves
- 2 amaretti cookies, crushed
- ¼ cup Parmesan cheese

Instructions:

1. Cook ravioli until al dente.
2. Melt butter and fry sage leaves until crispy.
3. Toss ravioli in butter and sprinkle with amaretti crumbs and Parmesan.

Spaghetti alla Puttanesca

Ingredients:

- 12 oz spaghetti
- 2 cloves garlic, minced
- ½ teaspoon red pepper flakes
- ½ cup Kalamata olives, sliced
- 2 tablespoons capers
- 1 can diced tomatoes
- 2 tablespoons olive oil
- ¼ cup chopped parsley

Instructions:

1. Cook spaghetti until al dente.
2. Sauté garlic, red pepper flakes, olives, and capers in olive oil.
3. Add tomatoes and simmer for 10 minutes.
4. Toss with pasta and garnish with parsley.

Busiate with Pesto Trapanese (Sicilian Almond Pesto)

Ingredients:

- 12 oz busiate pasta
- 2 cups cherry tomatoes
- ½ cup almonds
- 2 cloves garlic
- ½ cup basil leaves
- ¼ cup Parmesan cheese
- ½ cup olive oil

Instructions:

1. Blend tomatoes, almonds, garlic, basil, cheese, and olive oil into a pesto.
2. Cook busiate pasta until al dente, then toss with pesto.

Tagliatelle with Lemon and Shrimp

Ingredients:

- 12 oz tagliatelle
- ½ lb shrimp, peeled
- 1 lemon, zested and juiced
- 2 tablespoons butter
- 1 tablespoon olive oil
- ¼ teaspoon red pepper flakes
- ¼ cup Parmesan cheese

Instructions:

1. Cook tagliatelle until al dente.
2. Sauté shrimp, red pepper flakes, and lemon zest in butter and olive oil.
3. Toss with pasta, lemon juice, and Parmesan.

Cappelletti in Brodo (Stuffed Pasta in Broth)

Ingredients:

- 12 oz fresh cappelletti pasta
- 4 cups chicken broth
- 1 bay leaf
- ¼ teaspoon black pepper

Instructions:

1. Heat broth with bay leaf and black pepper.
2. Add cappelletti and cook for 5 minutes.
3. Serve hot with grated Parmesan.

Linguine with Lobster Sauce

Ingredients:

- 12 oz linguine
- 1 lobster tail, chopped
- 2 cloves garlic, minced
- 1 can diced tomatoes
- ½ teaspoon red pepper flakes
- ½ cup white wine
- 2 tablespoons olive oil

Instructions:

1. Cook linguine until al dente.
2. Sauté garlic and red pepper flakes in olive oil. Add lobster and white wine, cooking for 2 minutes.
3. Stir in tomatoes and simmer for 10 minutes.
4. Toss with pasta before serving.

Casunziei (Beet Ravioli from Veneto)

Ingredients:

- **For the pasta:**
    - 2 cups all-purpose flour
    - 2 eggs
    - 1 tablespoon olive oil
    - ½ teaspoon salt
- **For the filling:**
    - 1 cup cooked beets, mashed
    - ½ cup ricotta cheese
    - ¼ cup Parmesan cheese, grated
    - ½ teaspoon nutmeg
    - Salt and pepper to taste
- **For the sauce:**
    - 4 tablespoons butter
    - 6 fresh sage leaves
    - ¼ cup poppy seeds

Instructions:

1. Make pasta dough, knead, and let rest for 30 minutes.
2. Mix beets, ricotta, Parmesan, nutmeg, salt, and pepper for the filling.
3. Roll out dough and cut into circles. Place filling, fold into half-moons, and seal edges.
4. Boil for 3 minutes.
5. Melt butter with sage and toss ravioli, then sprinkle with poppy seeds.

Gramigna with Sausage and Saffron Cream

Ingredients:

- 12 oz gramigna pasta
- ½ lb Italian sausage, crumbled
- 1 small onion, diced
- ½ cup heavy cream
- ½ teaspoon saffron threads, soaked in warm water
- 2 tablespoons olive oil
- ¼ cup Parmesan cheese, grated

Instructions:

1. Cook gramigna until al dente.
2. Sauté sausage and onion in olive oil until browned.
3. Stir in cream and saffron water, simmer for 2 minutes.
4. Toss with pasta and sprinkle with Parmesan.

Tortellini alla Panna (Creamy Tortellini)

Ingredients:

- 12 oz fresh tortellini (cheese or meat-filled)
- 1 cup heavy cream
- ½ cup Parmesan cheese, grated
- 2 tablespoons butter
- ¼ teaspoon black pepper

Instructions:

1. Cook tortellini until al dente.
2. Heat butter and cream, then stir in Parmesan and pepper.
3. Toss with tortellini and serve.

Fusilli with Ricotta and Zucchini

Ingredients:

- 12 oz fusilli pasta
- 2 small zucchinis, diced
- 1 cup ricotta cheese
- 2 cloves garlic, minced
- 2 tablespoons olive oil
- ¼ cup Parmesan cheese, grated

Instructions:

1. Cook fusilli until al dente.
2. Sauté zucchini and garlic in olive oil.
3. Toss with pasta, ricotta, and Parmesan.

Agnolotti del Plin (Stuffed Pasta from Piedmont)

Ingredients:

- **For the pasta:**
    - 2 cups all-purpose flour
    - 2 eggs
    - ½ teaspoon salt
- **For the filling:**
    - ½ cup roasted veal or pork, minced
    - ½ cup ricotta cheese
    - ¼ cup Parmesan cheese, grated
    - 1 egg yolk
    - Salt and pepper to taste

Instructions:

1. Make pasta dough, knead, and let rest for 30 minutes.
2. Mix filling ingredients and set aside.
3. Roll out dough and cut into small squares, place filling, fold over, and pinch closed.
4. Boil for 3 minutes and serve with butter and sage.

Lasagna al Pesto

Ingredients:

- 12 lasagna sheets
- 1 cup basil pesto
- 1 cup ricotta cheese
- 1 cup béchamel sauce
- ½ cup mozzarella cheese, shredded
- ½ cup Parmesan cheese, grated

Instructions:

1. Preheat oven to 375°F (190°C).
2. Layer lasagna sheets, pesto, ricotta, and béchamel.
3. Repeat layers and top with mozzarella and Parmesan.
4. Bake for 30–35 minutes.

Pasta alla Gricia (Pecorino and Guanciale)

Ingredients:

- 12 oz rigatoni or tonnarelli
- 4 oz guanciale, diced
- 1 cup Pecorino Romano, grated
- ½ teaspoon black pepper

Instructions:

1. Cook pasta until al dente, reserving ½ cup pasta water.
2. Sauté guanciale until crispy.
3. Toss pasta with guanciale, black pepper, and Pecorino, adding pasta water to create a creamy sauce.

www.ingramcontent.com/pod-product-compliance
Lightning Source LLC
LaVergne TN
LVHW081506060526
838201LV00056BA/2965